FINDING PROMISED BLESSINGS ON THE COVENANT PATH

OTHER COVENANT BOOKS AND AUDIOBOOKS BY KERRY MUHLESTEIN

Return Unto Me

Scripture Study Made Simple: The Old Testament

The Essential Old Testament Companion

God Will Prevail: Ancient Prophets, Modern Blessings, and the Gathering of Israel

Learning to Love Isaiah

KERRY MUHLESTEIN

FINDING PROMISED BLESSINGS ON THE COVENANT PATH

Covenant Communications, Inc.

Cover image: *He Leadeth Me* © Yongsung Kim. Visit www.havenlight.com/collections/yongsung-kim for information on prints.

Cover design copyright © 2023 by Covenant Communications, Inc.
Cover design by Kevin Jorgensen

Published by Covenant Communications, Inc.
American Fork, Utah

Printed in the United States of America
First Printing: January 2023

32 31 30 29 28 27 26 25 24 23 10 9 8 7 6 5 4 3 2

ISBN 978-1-52442-383-4

Our covenant with God is of transcendent significance. Increasingly, Church leaders are emphasizing the spiritual significance of the covenant path. In a recent general conference address, President Russell M. Nelson spoke of getting on the covenant path and staying there, the first step toward gaining spiritual momentum, which "can help us withstand the relentless, wicked attacks of the adversary and thwart his efforts to erode our personal spiritual foundation." President Nelson further reminds us that as we move forward on the covenant path, we will have "greater strength to resist temptation, more peace of mind, freedom from fear, and greater unity in [our] families."[1] He also promised peace and rest for those who stay on the path by keeping their covenants.[2] Elder D. Todd Christofferson teaches that this path is "the *one* path that leads to the celestial kingdom of God."[3]

Surely, we all desire the blessings President Nelson promises and the joy of gaining the celestial kingdom of which Elder Christofferson speaks, all of which hinges upon our staying on the covenant path. But what is that path, and how can we tell if we are still on it? What does that look like in everyday life for us? How should our desire to stay on that path affect our actions and thoughts? What is the relationship between our baptismal and temple covenants, the new and everlasting covenant, and the Abrahamic covenant?

---

1 Russell M. Nelson, "The Power of Spiritual Momentum," *Liahona,* May 2022, 98.

2 Russell M. Nelson, "Overcome the World and Find Rest," general conference, October 2022.

3 D. Todd Christofferson, "Why the Covenant Path," *Liahona,* May 2021, 116; emphasis added.

Are these the same covenant, or are they different agreements? If they are different, do they each have their own path? Further, we may be asking how we can best find the blessings promised to Israel that President Nelson has asked us to find. And how can we find those blessings in the scriptures if we don't recognize the covenant in the scriptures as well as we should? How do we know when God is promising blessings to Israel, and how does becoming familiar with covenant language in the scriptures help us to better recognize His promises?

Many of us have pondered at least a few of these questions as we hear repeatedly about the importance of the covenant path. Not being sure of the answer to these questions can cause us to worry about our ability to recognize the steps on that path and thrive as we travel along it. It can also hamper our abilities to follow President Nelson's admonition to search for the blessings promised to Israel.

This booklet is designed to help you through a simple three-step plan:

1. We will briefly outline what the covenant is.
2. We will outline many of the blessings that the scriptures promise as part of the covenant, which will help us fulfill President Nelson's invitation to make a list of the blessings promised to the children of Israel. Further, we will try to help you develop skills in recognizing promised covenant blessings.
3. We will then discuss what staying on the covenant path looks like and how it should impact us.

What Is the Covenant?

President Nelson has taught us that the Abrahamic covenant and the new and everlasting covenant are the same thing.[4] Further, he has asked us to focus on keeping that covenant and recognizing the blessings that come from doing so.[5] This suggests that

4 Russell M. Nelson, "The Everlasting Covenant," *Liahona,* October 2022, 4.

5 See Russell M. Nelson, "Thanks for the Covenant" (Brigham Young University devotional address, November 22, 1988), speeches.byu.edu; see also Russell M. Nelson, "Let God Prevail," *Ensign* or *Liahona*, November 2020, 95.

understanding the Abrahamic covenant can help us know what the covenant path is and thus better enable us to stay on it. It will also help us to recognize the blessings promised to Israel. Yet sometimes we feel we don't fully understand the promises made to Abraham, and as a result it seems all the more confusing as we try to make sure we are on a covenant path that may consist of things we don't know about. We find ourselves in a quandary: we feel it is imperative to make sure we are on the covenant path, but what exactly is that covenant? Further, if we don't know what it is, how can we be sure we are on its path? If we aren't sure about that, how can we know how to pursue it wholeheartedly and with full confidence that we can do so?

Let us be clear. We enter into the Abrahamic covenant—also known as the new and everlasting covenant, or the covenant path—at baptism.[6] Many people may somewhat partake of that holy agreement by being born into a family that has made those promises. Yet to be fully immersed in the covenant, we must individually choose to enter into it. When we do so, we take upon ourselves specific obligations, which, if we honor them, will yield a multitude of specific blessings.

This bond with God, with its obligations and blessings, is broadened, or reemphasized and clarified, in the temple. Our initiatory ordinances are really further pronouncements of covenantal blessings, and they echo our baptismal covenant in many ways. The temple endowment and the sealing ceremony continue to expand the covenant, helping us to better understand it and thus prepare us for further blessings. Fortunately, we can renew all these covenants—better stated as all these elements of The Covenant—weekly as we partake of the sacrament.

With this general understanding of how we enter into the covenant, let us look at its specifics. We will look at the blessings we receive from entering into this bond with God and the obligations we must meet if we are to receive those blessings.

---

6 Nelson, "The Everlasting Covenant," 4, 6. For more on this, see Kerry Muhlestein, *God Will Prevail: Ancient Covenants, Modern Blessings, and the Gathering of Israel* (American Fork, UT: Covenant Communications, 2021), 4–7.

Promise of Personal Relationship

Our understanding of the covenant and our ability to recognize whether or not we are on the covenant path are greatly increased when we remember that the central feature of the Abrahamic covenant and its attendant path is God's desire to have a closer relationship with us. Everything else in the covenant—or plan—hinges on the concept of having a heightened bond with God. It was God's yearning to amplify our relationship with Him that caused Him to create the covenant, and every element He put into that bond stems from this divine desire. Knowing this should influence the way we think about all aspects of the covenant.

In some ways, this special bond is summed up in the Hebrew word *hesed.* This word denotes a special kind of love, loyalty, and mercy available only within a covenant. Speaking of *hesed,* President Nelson teaches, "Once you and I have made a covenant with God, our relationship with him becomes much closer than before our covenant. Now we are bound together."[7]

As Elder Christofferson teaches, "The covenants God offers to His children do more than guide us. They bind us to Him."[8] Similarly, Elder David A. Bednar reminds us, "Entering into sacred covenants and worthily receiving priesthood ordinances yoke us with and bind us to the Lord Jesus Christ and Heavenly Father."[9] He further explains, "Living and loving covenant commitments creates a connection with the Lord that is deeply personal and spiritually powerful. As we honor the conditions of sacred covenants and ordinances, we gradually and incrementally are drawn closer to Him and experience the impact of His divinity and living reality in our lives."[10]

As part of increasing this relationship, we promise to love God more than anyone or anything else—to have Him prevail in our lives

---

7 Nelson, "The Everlasting Covenant," 6. See also Muhlestein, *God Will Prevail,* 9–12.

8 Christofferson, "Why the Covenant Path," 118.

9 David A. Bednar, "But We Heeded Them Not," *Liahona*, May 2022, 15.

10 Bednar, "But We Heeded Them Not," 15.

more than any other thing.[11] We also pledge to love His children. In return, God promises to send His Spirit to be with us, which will sanctify us, or change who we are, making us godlier and thus more capable of experiencing a closer relationship with our Father. This can happen because of the atoning sacrifice of His Son, Jesus Christ, who was sent to make it possible for the covenant blessings to be fulfilled.

There are ways that we must act in order to take full advantage of the sanctifying power of Christ's atoning sacrifice as carried into our souls by the Holy Ghost. God teaches us how to act in a godlier way by giving us commandments. Many of these commandments are given to us by prophets, both ancient and modern. Some are given to us individually through the Holy Ghost. When we enter into our covenant with God, we promise to obey His commands and instructions. Loving Him makes it natural for us to want to obey (see John 14:15). All of this is the natural outcome of having the kind of closer relationship with God that is forged through a covenant. While we have always known we must obey commandments, it is useful—and even transformative—to have at the forefront of our mind this connection between relationships, covenants, and commandments.

One of the many reasons God sent His Son to earth was so that Christ could serve as an exemplar. Thus, Christ's life serves as another way for us to know how to act in a godly manner. Again, following that example takes on added meaning when we focus on how it helps us fulfill covenants and thus heightens our relationship with God. We will discuss this further when we speak of the covenant path below.

The close bond between a covenant holder and God naturally yields a number of blessings. Becoming godlier, or holy, allows us to have better and more frequent communication with God. This creates another upward cycle as He directs us more and more and as we act on those directions. The blessings are two-fold: we act more and more godly and thus make ourselves more available to Him so

11 See Nelson, "Let God Prevail," 94.

that we can have our natures changed incrementally to a state similar to God's. This increased unity of nature and communion creates a crescendoing intimate bond that allows us to experience God's presence even more fully. This happens both in terms of having the Holy Ghost with us to direct, comfort, and change us, and in terms of receiving ordinances that bring God into our lives. It also allows us to more fully experience His presence in our chapels, temples, and homes, which are dedicated to Him. All these things allow us to be spiritually begotten of God, which is part of the change we are hoping for.[12] We are reminded of the bonding experience of King Benjamin's people when they entered into a covenant with Christ. "And now, because of the covenant which ye have made ye shall be called the children of Christ, his sons, and his daughters; for behold, this day he hath spiritually begotten you; for ye say that your hearts are changed through faith on his name; therefore, ye are born of him and have become his sons and his daughters" (Mosiah 5:7).

Promise of Protection

Of course, when two beings have a close relationship with greater union, communion, and ability to share power and direction, some other things will naturally flow from that relationship. Just as spouses naturally feel protective toward their covenant partner, and as parents naturally feel protective toward their children, and just as being together so much allows them to better protect each other, so God can better protect His children who have entered into a covenant relationship with Him. Some of that protection comes in the form of the higher communion, which such bonded partners have with each other; for protection often takes the form of God communicating crucial information or warnings to us. There are many other ways that covenant children can be protected by God.

---

12 This paragraph and the following six paragraphs are a very slightly modified version of part of an online essay I wrote. See Kerry Muhlestein, "The Abrahamic Covenant, Its Influence on Scriptures, and What that Has to Do with Us," *Come, Follow Me Thoughts to Keep in Mind* (blog), FAIR, February 6, 2022, https://www.fairlatterdaysaints.org/blog/2022/02/06/come-follow-me-thoughts-to-keep-in-mind-the-covenant.

This promise of protection does not mean that no harm will ever come to those who are ensconced in the covenant, for that would contravene the conditions necessary for us to have a successful mortal probation. As President Nelson teaches, "Returning to the covenant path does *not* mean that life will be easy. This path is rigorous and at times will feel like a steep climb. This ascent, however, is designed to test and teach us, refine our natures, and help us to become saints. It is the *only* path that leads to exaltation."[13] Painful and tragic things will happen to everyone, including covenant keepers. Still, these challenges will be less difficult than they would be without the promised blessings, and all bad things will eventually be conquered and ended for covenant holders. We can be sure, however, that ultimately everything that besets us, every kind of bedevilment, ailment, and scourge, including even death and hell, will be overcome as we find ourselves behind the protective shield of our mighty God. President Nelson promises that those who cherish their covenant above all other commitments and who let God prevail in their lives will experience "greater peace, confidence, joy, and yes, rest."[14]

Promise of Prosperity

Great prosperity is another natural outgrowth of increased union and communion with God. When we hear God more, and when we are experiencing His power and trying to live as He asks, and are being changed by Him, then prosperity naturally follows. It comes abundantly because of God's powerful involvement in every aspect of our lives and His ability to magnify every good thing we do. It also follows as a natural consequence of acting in a godlier way—elsewise stated as acting in a way that is in harmony with eternal truths. This prosperity is often scripturally described in terms of abundant yields coming from our labors (see for example Leviticus 26:4–5 and Deuteronomy 28:3–6, 8, 11–12). Yet it also comes in terms of spiritual, mental, emotional, and physical prosperity.

13 Nelson, "The Power of Spiritual Momentum," 99.

14 Nelson, "Overcome the World and Find Rest," October 2022 general conference.

Such prosperity is an oft-repeated promise in both the Old Testament and the Book of Mormon. Again, this does not mean that covenant holders will never experience any lack of prosperity. Physical, financial, emotional, and spiritual trials are bound to come; they are necessary aspects of our mortal probation. They may even last for devastatingly significant periods of time, despite our faithful keeping of the covenant. Yet the promise of overall prosperity is sure, and full faith in that promise should help us get through the times when we are not experiencing it. As Elder Bednar teaches, "I frankly do not have the ability to describe adequately the precise nature and power of our covenant connection with the resurrected and living Son of God. But I witness that the connections with Him and Heavenly Father are real and are the ultimate sources of assurance, peace, joy, and the spiritual strength that enable us to 'fear not, though the enemy deride.'"[15] Surely at least some of this comfort comes from feeling deep within our soul—at the core of how we think of ourselves—the strength of our covenant-enhanced relationship with God. This leads to a stronger confidence in His promises of protection and prosperity. Indeed, Elder Bednar tells us of Saints who "speak of covenants providing strength to overcome opposition and their connection with the living Lord supporting them through times both good and bad."[16] As President Nelson has taught, though we can expect opposition on the path, covenant keepers can "find true rest, meaning relief and peace, even amid your most vexing problems."[17]

Promise of Posterity

The ultimate form of prosperity is to have bountiful and beautiful posterity. This can take many forms and is fulfilled over a long period of time. One obvious form is to have children with whom we can develop close relationships. For *some* that will happen in this life; for *all* covenant keepers it will happen most fully in the next life. Abinadi tells us that one of the most important

15 Bednar, "But We Heeded Them Not," 15.

16 Bednar, "But We Heeded Them Not," 15.

17 Nelson, "Overcome the World and Find Rest," October 2022 general conference.

ways the promise of posterity is fulfilled is when we help someone come to Christ to receive the kind of covenantal life He can give them; those people then become our seed (see Mosiah 15:10–17). Undoubtedly there are many other ways this promise is fulfilled that we cannot foresee. The promise of numerous posterity is one of the most joyous and important blessings assured to those who have bound themselves to God.

Promise of Place

Of course, prosperity and abundant posterity cannot happen if there is no place for covenant families to thrive. Therefore, having a place, or a promised land, is an essential part of the promised blessings. Such a promised land can take several different forms. Often it means having a literal land in which covenant holders can live together. There they will have a place for their plenteous children to grow and live. They will also have a land that can yield the food necessary for such abundant life.

As covenant keepers, we need the protection that is promised us, for the other blessings that flow from our bond with God will encourage both men and Satan to beset us. Our prosperity will set us apart and engender some jealousy. When anyone lives in a place that is yielding abundantly, then others will want to take that land and prosperity from them, which makes the promise of protection even more salient. Land, prosperity, posterity, and protection are all integrally tied together. The promise of land will not last if not accompanied by protection.

A literal promised land has often proved to be crucial for the spread of the covenant and for the prosperity of the posterity of Israel. We can see the need for a literal promised land in the history of ancient Israel. We also see that need in the history of modern restored Israel in the early generations of the Restoration. The Saints repeatedly tried to gather, only to be persecuted and chased from place to place. Yet today we gather to different kinds of places. We gather to our temples and our meetinghouses and our homes. These are also fulfillments of the promise of a land or a place. We are so blessed by the fact that at home or wherever we travel we can find a group of Saints with whom we can immediately bond, and thus we can have a "place" to belong. The more of us who are trying to keep our covenants—or live celestially—the more ways we will find the promise of a place being fulfilled. The ultimate fulfillment of this is the true promised land, or the celestial kingdom.

Promise of Exaltation

The notion of the true promised land highlights the greatest promise that flows from our heightened relationship with God. The opportunity to gain the true promised land (the celestial kingdom) flows from all the above promises in this way: Our union with God yields a) an increased communication, which yields b) knowledge of how to approach Him, which causes c) His power to be manifested in our lives and our beings, so that d) we prosper by being changed, and thus become spiritually more like Him. The combination of those blessings makes it easier for us to receive e) His protection from all that besets us, including death and hell. All of this eventually brings us to f) the true promised land and promised state of being. In other words, it brings us to *exaltation*. As Elder Christofferson teaches, "It is only in pursuing the covenant path that we inherit the blessings of Abraham, Isaac, and Jacob, the ultimate blessings of salvation and exaltation that only God can give."[18] We must never forget that these blessings, including exaltation, can only happen because Christ kept His covenant and went through His atoning sacrifice for us. It is remarkable to think that if we are doing our best to keep our covenant, we are promised a full, beautiful, and unimaginably glorious exaltation.

The reception of any promised blessings is contingent upon our coming to Christ and fulfilling our covenant obligations. As noted above, these obligations primarily consist of loving God, loving His children, and obeying His instructions as to how to behave in a godly way—also known as commandments. Loving God and His children naturally leads to another of our great obligations: we are

18 Christofferson, "Why the Covenant Path," 118.

to share His covenant with others. This helps all of His children gather back to God. President Nelson has taught that this gathering is the most important work on earth.[19] He has further explained that anytime we do anything to help people make and keep covenants, on either side of the veil, we are actively helping with this magnificent work of gathering.[20] As we fulfill our obligations, we will increasingly experience the promised blessings until we receive the fullness of those blessings; meaning, until our natures become godly—or Christlike—and we receive exaltation in the celestial kingdom, where we will enjoy our Father's presence and never again have to lose it.

Blessings Promised to Israel

It should be clear that the blessings available through this covenant are supernal. President Russell M. Nelson promises, "Your commitment to follow the Savior by making covenants with Him and then keeping those covenants will open the door to every spiritual blessing and privilege available to men, women, and children everywhere."[21] Later, in the October 2020 general conference, he asked us to pursue a course of study that would help us to better understand these blessings.[22] He said, "As you study your scriptures during the next six months, I encourage you to make a list of all that the Lord has promised He will do for covenant Israel. I think you will be astounded! Ponder these promises. Talk about them with your family and friends. Then live and watch for these promises to be fulfilled in your own life."[23]

---

19 See Russell M. Nelson and Wendy W. Nelson, "Hope of Israel" (worldwide youth devotional, June 3, 2018), supplement to the *New Era* and *Ensign*, ChurchofJesusChrist.org.

20 See Nelson and Nelson, "Hope of Israel."

21 Russell M. Nelson, "As We Go Forward Together," *Ensign* or *Liahona*, April 2018, 7.

22 The next few paragraphs are a modified version of part of an article I published. See Kerry Muhlestein, "The Unique Relationship with God We are Promised in the Covenant," *Meridian Magazine*, February 25, 2021, https://latterdaysaintmag.com/the-unique-relationship-with-god-we-are-promised-in-the-covenant/.

23 Nelson, "Let God Prevail," 95.

Just one year prior to this, he asked the Saints to study the First Vision.[24] It seems to me that we responded to this request with vigor. I believe we have wanted to respond with the same vigor in looking for the blessings promised to Israel, but it has been more difficult. Most found it somewhat easy to find accounts of the First Vision and study them. In contrast, I have found that members of The Church of Jesus Christ of Latter-day Saints have a more difficult time recognizing the blessings promised to Israel while studying their scriptures. As a result, it has not been as easy to wholeheartedly follow the prophet's advice this time. Wherever I have traveled to teach on this topic, I have found a degree of desperation as people have tried to rise to the prophet's invitations but have not been sure whether or not they are succeeding. At the same time, during all these travels, I have found people who, after being taught how to find these blessings in the scriptures, have felt like the scriptures have opened up to them in an entirely new and exhilarating way.

One crucial element of moving from invitation consternation to invitation elation is to become familiar with the Abrahamic covenant and the language used to describe it, and then recognize that language in the scriptures. The first step is to study passages where the covenant is discussed at some length. There are a few places in the scriptures where we can find the blessings promised to Israel packed densely into a chapter or two, and I recommend taking some time to study those passages. For example, Genesis 12, 15 and 17; Abraham 2; Leviticus 26; or Deuteronomy 28–30 are all chapters where the covenant and its blessings are powerfully discussed. Studying these chapters allows us to become familiar enough with the covenant to start to recognize when the scriptures are speaking of the blessings associated with it. In order to help you, below is a chart highlighting the blessings as outlined in Leviticus 26 and Deuteronomy 28–30. I recommend that you study those chapters using the chart as a guide, and then read Genesis 12, 15, 17, and Abraham 2 and create a similar list or chart on your own. This will be good practice in recognizing the blessings of the covenant.

---

24 See Russell M. Nelson, "Closing Remarks," *Ensign* or *Liahona*, November 2019, 122.

Leviticus Blessings	Deuteronomy Blessings
If ye walk in my statutes, and keep my commandments, and do them (Leviticus 26:3).	If thou shalt hearken diligently unto the voice of the Lord thy God, to observe and to do all his commandments which I command thee this day (Deuteronomy 28:1). If that thou hearken unto the commandments of the Lord thy God, which I command thee this day, to observe and to do them (Deuteronomy 28:13).
Ye shall make you no idols nor graven image, neither rear you up a standing image, neither shall ye set up any image of stone in your land, to bow down unto it: for I am the Lord your God (Leviticus 26:1).	And thou shalt not go aside from any of the words which I command thee this day, to the right hand, or to the left, to go after other gods to serve them (Deuteronomy 28:14).
Then I will give you rain in due season, and the land shall yield her increase, and the trees of the field shall yield their fruit. And your threshing shall reach unto the vintage, and the vintage shall reach unto the sowing time: and ye shall eat your bread to the full (Leviticus 26:4–5). And ye shall eat old store, and bring forth the old because of the new (Leviticus 26:10).	Blessings shall come on thee, and overtake thee . . . Blessed shalt thou be in the city, and blessed shalt thou be in the field. . . . Blessed shall be . . . the fruit of thy ground, and the fruit of thy cattle, the increase of thy kine, and the flocks of thy sheep. Blessed shall be thy basket and thy store (Deuteronomy 28:2–5). The Lord shall command the blessing upon thee in thy storehouses, and in all that thou settest thine hand unto (Deuteronomy 28:8). And the Lord shall make thee plenteous in goods, in the fruit of thy body, and in the fruit of thy cattle, and in the fruit of thy ground. . . . The Lord shall open unto thee his good treasure, the heaven to give the rain unto thy land in his season, and to bless all the work of thine hand: and thou shalt lend unto many nations, and thou shalt not borrow (Deuteronomy 28:11–12).

For I will have respect unto you, and make you fruitful, and multiply you, and establish my covenant with you (Leviticus 26:9).	Blessed shall be the fruit of thy body (Deuteronomy 28:4).
[You will] dwell in your land safely. And I will give peace in the land (Leviticus 26:5–6).	He shall bless thee in the land which the Lord thy God giveth thee (Deuteronomy 28:8). And the Lord shall make thee plenteous . . . in the land which the Lord sware unto thy fathers to give thee (Deuteronomy 28:11).
Ye shall lie down, and none shall make you afraid: and I will rid evil beasts out of the land, neither shall the sword go through your land. And ye shall chase your enemies, and they shall fall before you by the sword. And five of you shall chase an hundred, and an hundred of you shall put ten thousand to flight: and your enemies shall fall before you by the sword (Leviticus 26:6–8).	The Lord shall cause thine enemies that rise up against thee to be smitten before thy face: they shall come out against thee one way, and flee before thee seven ways (Deuteronomy 28:7). And all the people of the earth shall see that thou art called by the name of the Lord; and they shall be afraid of thee (Deuteronomy 28:10).
And I will set my tabernacle among you: and my soul shall not abhor you. And I will walk among you, and will be your God, and ye shall be my people (Leviticus 26:11–12).	The Lord shall establish thee an holy people unto himself (Deuteronomy 28:9).
I am the Lord your God, which brought you forth out of the land of Egypt, that ye should not be their bondmen; and I have broken the bands of your yoke, and made you go upright (Leviticus 26:13).	And the Lord shall make thee the head, and not the tail; and thou shalt be above only, and thou shalt not be beneath (Deuteronomy 28:13).

If we want to find the blessings promised to Israel in the scriptures, as President Nelson asked us to, then learning to recognize these most prominent covenantal promises and looking for times when those concepts are referred to in the scriptures will be immensely helpful.

Textual Cues Pointing to the Covenant

The most commonly used textual cues include the following:[25]

1. The phrase "my people" or a variant thereof[26]
2. The phrase "your god" or a variant thereof[27]
3. References to multiplying or becoming populous[28]
4. References to (re)inheriting land[29]
5. References to conquering enemies or being protected from enemies[30]
6. References to prosperity in the promised land[31]
7. References to self-rulership[32]
8. References to enjoying God's presence in a house of God[33]
9. References to the fathers, or promises made to the fathers[34]
10. References to God helping those who have broken the covenant find a way to return to it[35]

25 This list comes from the article by Kerry Muhlestein, "Recognizing the Everlasting Covenant in the Scriptures," *Religious Educator*, vol. 21, no. 2 (2020), 52. The previous chart is a modified version of the chart in that article (46–49).

26 For each of these motifs, a few scriptural references for when those promises are made as part of the covenant will be included. For this one, see Exodus 6:7; Leviticus 26:12; Deuteronomy 7:6; 28:9–10; and 29:13.

27 Genesis 17:7, 8; Exodus 6:7; Leviticus 26:12; Deuteronomy 29:13; Abraham 1:19; and Abraham 2:7.

28 Genesis 13:16; 15:5; 17:2, 4–6; 22:17; 24:60; Leviticus 26:9; Deuteronomy 6:3; 30:16; Abraham 2:9; and 3:14.

29 Genesis 12:1, 7; 13:15; 13:17; 15:7, 16, 18; 17:8; Exodus 6:8; Leviticus 18:24–30; 25:18; Deuteronomy 5:33; 6:1, 18; 30:16, 20; Abraham 2:6, 19; and Doctrine and Covenants 52:2.

30 Genesis 22:17; 24:60; 15:1; Leviticus 25:18; and 26:5–7.

31 Genesis 15:1; 17:6; Leviticus 25:18–19; 26:4–5; Deuteronomy 6:3; 28:3–6, 8, 11–12; 29:9; 30:9, 16; and Abraham 2:9.

32 Genesis 17:6, 16; and Abraham 1:2.

33 Leviticus 26:11–12.

34 Genesis 17:4–5; 26:25; Abraham 1:2–4.

35 Leviticus 26:41–46; 1 Kings 8:46–51; 1 Nephi 2:24.

"My People" as an Indicator of Covenant Blessings

Let's look at some of the blessings promised to Israel that we can find when we recognize these textual clues. To begin with, let's look at what we can learn of Christ and His atoning sacrifice when we keep an eye out for the phrase "my people" or "his people." I have studied these phrases carefully over a number of years. As far as I can tell, *every time* these phrases are used, they are referring to people who have entered into a covenant with God.

We know and understand that Christ suffered for all God's children. Surely His atoning sacrifice was wrought for all humanity. While we recognize this profound truth, we must be careful not to impose upon scriptural teachings our own understanding of what and for whom Christ suffered. We are better served by letting the scriptures speak for themselves. While there are many places where we are taught that Christ suffered for all of mankind (see 1 Nephi 19:9; 2 Nephi 9:21–22 for example), there seem to be more scriptures that specify that His suffering was most specifically for God's covenant people. In at least one place, these groups are both spoken of at the same time (see Mosiah 3:7–11). It is important for us to allow the scriptures to tell us what they are trying to tell us rather than impose our own view upon them. As we explore this topic, we will see that the scriptural authors often speak of Christ's sufferings being for those who are in a covenant relationship with Him and His Father. This does not mean that His atoning sacrifice was not suffered for all mankind, but it does mean that there is something else He is trying to tell us, and we must pay careful attention to determine what that is.

In Isaiah 63, there are some beautiful descriptions of what God had done for Israel that are also symbolic of Christ's atoning sacrifice. The imagery therein is so applicable to our day that some of it was repeated in Doctrine and Covenants 133:50–53. In Isaiah 63:7, Isaiah speaks about Jehovah's "great goodness toward the house of Israel, which he hath bestowed on them according to his mercies, and according to the multitude of his lovingkindnesses." The word translated as "lovingkindness" is *hesed*, which is that kind of love and mercy that happens only within a covenant.[36] Between that phrase and the mention of the "house of Israel," we should be keyed in to the fact that God is speaking about blessings promised to His covenant people.

That thought continues through the next few verses. There the Lord says, "Surely, they are *my people*, children that will not lie: so he was their Saviour. In all their affliction he was afflicted, and the angel of his presence saved them: in his love and in his pity he redeemed them; and he bare them, and carried them all the days of old" (Isaiah 63:8–9; emphasis added). While the house of Israel is clearly referenced in verse 7, that reference is carried through to the next few verses by using the phrase *my people*, which means "people in a covenant relationship with me." Thus, these verses teach us that it is because of that forged relationship that He is afflicted for us and that He has saved and redeemed us in love and pity and carried us. Isaiah teaches this same idea ten chapters earlier, when he declares, "He was cut off out of the land of the living: for the transgression of *my people* was he stricken" (Isaiah 53:8; emphasis added; see also Mosiah 14:8). Here Isaiah makes it clear that Christ suffered for the transgressions of all those from all dispensations who would enter into and keep a covenant relationship with Him.

These are incredible blessings—blessings available to all covenant holders and keepers. It is important to remember that we plead with everyone to enter the covenant, desperately wanting for all of humanity to join in this relationship that offers such redeeming blessings. At the same time, in some ways, these verses are saying that the atoning sacrifice of Christ has its fullest efficacy for covenant keepers. Simultaneously, it assures us that all who enter into the covenant can and will receive the full blessings of Christ's atoning grace and power. Thus, we see the significance of both the infinite *and* intimate aspects of the Atonement.

This same sentiment is stated quite simply by Gabriel, as quoted in Matthew: "She shall bring forth a son, and thou shalt call his name Jesus: for he shall save *his people* from their sins" (Matthew 1:21; emphasis added). Zachariah, father of John the Baptist,

36 See Muhlestein, *God Will Prevail,* 9–12.

who was tutored by Gabriel, similarly taught, "Blessed be the Lord God of Israel; for he hath visited and redeemed *his people*" (Luke 1:68; emphasis added). Zachariah also taught that his son, John the Baptist, would "give knowledge of salvation unto *his people* by the remission of their sins" (Luke 1:77; emphasis added).

We find similar sentiments in the Book of Mormon. Sometimes it is stated quite simply, such as when Christ taught, "Behold, I am he who was prepared from the foundation of the world to redeem *my people*. Behold, I am Jesus Christ" (Ether 3:14; emphasis added).

Elsewhere, we learn more of the suffering involved in Christ's redeeming sacrifice. King Benjamin was taught about Christ's sacrifice by an angel. That divine messenger imparted one of the most complete descriptions of what Christ would suffer and do for us: "And lo, he shall suffer temptations, and pain of body, hunger, thirst, and fatigue, even more than man can suffer, except it be unto death; for behold, blood cometh from every pore, so great shall be his anguish for the wickedness and the abominations of *his people*" (Mosiah 3:7; emphasis added). It is significant to note that the great pain Christ would suffer was specifically because of and for "his people," or in other words, for those in a covenant relationship with Him. Again, we see that the suffering, and presumably the grace available because of that suffering, is specifically for all covenant keepers. What an incredible blessing!

This same sentiment is echoed by Alma, who taught that Christ would take upon Himself "the transgressions of *his people*" (Alma 34:8; emphasis added). Elsewhere, Alma taught that Christ "shall go forth, suffering pains and afflictions and temptations of every kind; and this that the word might be fulfilled which saith he will take upon him the pains and the sicknesses of *his people*. And he will take upon him death, that he may loose the bands of death which bind *his people*; and he will take upon him *their* infirmities, that his bowels may be filled with mercy, according to the flesh, that he may know according to the flesh how to succor *his people* according to *their* infirmities. Now the Spirit knoweth all things;

nevertheless the Son of God suffereth according to the flesh that he might take upon him the sins of *his people*, that he might blot out their transgressions according to the power of his deliverance" (Alma 7:11–13; emphasis added). In all of scripture, this is one of the most touching descriptions of Christ's suffering and the reasons for it. We learn that Christ suffered every kind of pain—from death to any and all kinds of infirmity. We further learn that He does so not only to release us from death, but also so that He can experience our pain in order to better succor "his people." And who are the "people" referred to in these verses? It is for those in a covenant relationship with Him—the suffering and the succoring is specifically for those willing to repent, accept the Savior's gift of amazing grace, and enter into a covenant with Him. Once again, we see both the infinite *and* intimate aspects of the Atonement. What a blessing! Surely Christ succors any who call upon Him, but these verses are specifically dedicated to describing the succoring that is available for covenant holders.

The blessing of the Resurrection, which is possible because of Christ's atoning sacrifice, is universally available. Repentance, succoring, comfort, and a host of other blessings that come from Christ's sufferings are also available to all. At the same time, the fullest blessings that come from Christ's atoning sacrifice, those of full sanctification and exaltation, and surely some degree of succoring, are available only to those who make and strive to keep covenants. This may be why the scriptures most often speak of the blessings of the Atonement in terms of its application to covenant keepers. It is surely also part of why the Father and Son are so anxious that covenant holders do all they can to invite others on both sides of the veil to join the covenant. While God consistently speaks of a difference between those who have made covenants and those who have not, He absolutely does not want us to think of this in terms of an "us" and "them" mentality. Instead, He insists that we must think of our fellow mortals in terms of "How can we get them to join us, to belong with us?" As we more fully experience the sanctifying and transformative blessings of the covenant, we will feel an even stronger desire to have everyone join us in that covenant so they can fully receive all its blessings, most especially the blessings that flow from Christ's atoning sacrifice to His people. Those blessings are real, and are consistently and frequently described in the scriptures.

What a gift it is to understand the connection—clearly and beautifully described by ancient prophets—between Christ's covenant with us and His atoning sufferings and sacrifice. We can fully appreciate this only when we are simultaneously looking for the blessings promised to Israel and are becoming aware of the phrases that indicate that the covenant with Israel is being referenced. There are other places where the phrase *my people* or *his people* alerts us to blessings promised to the house of Israel. Below is a list of some of the places where we see blessings promised to God's (covenant) people. Sometimes the blessings listed are so similar that you will see several scriptural references that speak of that particular blessing, Yet at other times, God employs such beautiful and different language to describe the blessing that I list the same blessing separately so we can appreciate the wording that makes each somewhat unique.

God will see our bondage and affliction and come to deliver us

- Exodus 3:7–8; Psalm 59:11; Jeremiah 51:45; Mosiah 24:13–14, 16; Doctrine and Covenants 103:16–17

God will do marvels among us

- Exodus 34:10

God will be among us

- Leviticus 26:12

God will redeem us

- Deuteronomy 21:8; 1 Chronicles 17:21; Psalm 77:15; Isaiah 52:9; Mosiah 13:33; 15:1, 18–19; 16:4; Alma 5:21, 27; 6:8; 11:40; 33:22; Helaman 5:10; 3 Nephi 6:20; 16:19; 20:34; Ether 3:14; Doctrine and Covenants 84:99–101

After we are redeemed, we will reign with God

- Doctrine and Covenants 43:29; 84:119; 133:25

God will have mercy on us
- Deuteronomy 21:8; 32:43

God will bless us in our land
- Deuteronomy 26:15

God will avenge us
- Deuteronomy 32:43

God will deliver us from our enemies
- 1 Samuel 9:16; Doctrine and Covenants 101:10

God will not forsake us
- 1 Kings 6:13

God will answer our supplications
- 1 Kings 8:38–39

God will support us in our battles
- 1 Kings 8:44–49

God will forgive us
- 1 Kings 8:50; Doctrine and Covenants 109:34

God will give us rest
- 1 Kings 8:56; 1 Chronicles 23:25

We will have a place that is ours and from which we will not be removed
- 1 Chronicles 17:9

God will move our enemies from before us
- 1 Chronicles 17:21; Doctrine and Covenants 109:26–28

Land and enemies will be subdued for us
- 1 Chronicles 22:18

God will love us
- 2 Chronicles 2:11

God will hear us and forgive us if we humble ourselves and seek Him
- 2 Chronicles 7:14

We will have enough and more of what we need
- 2 Chronicles 31:10

God will have compassion on us and warn us when we need to repent

- 2 Chronicles 36:15

We will be blessed with salvation

- Psalm 3:8; Mosiah 15:18

We will have strength

- Psalm 29:11

We will have peace

- Psalm 29:11

God will march before us in our trials

- Psalm 68:7

God will bring us out of the places we have wandered and the trials we are in

- Psalm 68:22

We will receive strength and power from God

- Psalm 68:35

God will judge (or lead and make things right for) us with righteousness

- Psalm 72:2; 135:14

God will lead us back to promised lands and give us a full cup of blessings

- Psalm 73:10

God will speak peace to us

- Psalm 85:8

We will not be cast off

- Psalm 94:14

We will receive our inheritance

- Psalm 94:14

We will be multiplied and made stronger than our enemies

- Psalm 105:24

God will always be round about to protect His people

- Psalm 125:2

We will have a land, or place, for our heritage

- Psalm 135:12; Isaiah 60:21; Ezekiel 36:28; 3 Nephi 20:29, 46

God will always preserve a remnant of us

- Isaiah 10:22; Moses 7:61

God will always gather the preserved remnant back to Him

- Isaiah 11:11; 3 Nephi 20:18; 29; 21:1; Doctrine and Covenants 101:65

God will prepare a way for us to return to Him

- Isaiah 11:16; 57:14; 3 Nephi 24:16–18

We will have safe, peaceful places in which to dwell

- Isaiah 32:18

We will be comforted

- Isaiah 40:1; 49:13; 52:9; Mosiah 12:23; 15:30; 3 Nephi 16:19; 20:34

We will come to know God's name

- Isaiah 52:6; 3 Nephi 20:39

We will all be righteous

- Isaiah 60:21

God will save us (or be our Savior)

- Isaiah 63:8; Zechariah 8:8; Doctrine and Covenants 136:22

God will bring us joy

- Isaiah 65:18

God will rejoice in us

- Isaiah 65:19; Jeremiah 32:41

God will have mercy on us when we repent and will return us to our place of belonging and give us our heritage and keep covenant with us

- Jeremiah 12:14–15; Hosea 2:23

God will give us a heart to know Him

- Jeremiah 24:7

God will help us return to Him and keep our covenant with Him

- Jeremiah 24:7

God will bring us back to our place of belonging and our promises after we stray

- Jeremiah 30:3, 22

God will love us with an everlasting love and draw us to Him with lovingkindness

- Jeremiah 31:1–3

God will save us and gather us together

- Jeremiah 31:7–8

We will be satiated and satisfied with the goodness of God

- Jeremiah 31:14; Joel 2:18–19

We will have God's law written in our softened hearts

- Jeremiah 31:33

When God gathers us together after we stray, He will keep covenant with us and give us one heart

- Jeremiah 32:38–39; Hosea 2:23

God will plant us in our place of belonging with all his heart and soul

- Jeremiah 32:41

God will bring us all the good He has ever promised us

- Jeremiah 32:42

God will give us a softened and unified heart with a new spirit and keep covenant with us

- Ezekiel 11:19

God will deliver us from the hand of our enemies

- Ezekiel 13:23

God will deliver us from spiritual pollutions and bring us back to Him

- Ezekiel 14:11

We will dwell safely and prosperously
- Ezekiel 34:25–29

We will know that God is with us
- Ezekiel 34:30

The land will yield its fruit to us
- Ezekiel 36:8

God will multiply us and our fruits and our places to live and belong, and eventually we won't be bereaved
- Ezekiel 36:11–12

We will rise from the dead and receive our inheritance
- Ezekiel 37:12

God will save us from our sinful acts and cleanse us
- Ezekiel 37:23

We can experience God's presence in His house
- Ezekiel 37:27; Doctrine and Covenants 42:36; 97:15; 109:5, 11–12; 110:6–8

We will know the name of God and not pollute it
- Ezekiel 39:7

Eventually we will not be scattered from our place or possessions
- Ezekiel 46:18

We will be called by God's name and will belong to Him
- Daniel 9:19

We will eat in plenty and be satisfied, and God will deal wondrously with us and we will not be ashamed
- Joel 2:26–27

God will be our hope and our strength
- Joel 3:16

God will bring us out of captivity and give us wondrous prosperity and places
- Amos 9:14

God will save us and we will be the stones of His crown

- Zechariah 9:16

God will refine us

- Zechariah 13:9

God cannot cast us away

- Romans 11:1–2

God will dwell in us

- 2 Corinthians 6:16

God will destroy the great and abominable church to fulfill His covenants with us

- 1 Nephi 14:17

God will raise up Christ and prophets to give us guidance, deliverance, and salvation

- 1 Nephi 22:20; 2 Nephi 3:9, 15; Doctrine and Covenants 103:16

God will make the gospel available to us

- 2 Nephi 31:3; Doctrine and Covenants 10:52

Christ will manifest Himself unto us

- 2 Nephi 25:17

We will have opportunity to know about Christ

- 2 Nephi 26:3

God will not forget us, but will gather us in to Himself whenever we have strayed

- 2 Nephi 29:1–2; Doctrine and Covenants 29:2; 39:11

God will gather us to a place and to Himself and will fight our enemies for us

- 2 Nephi 29:14; 30:8–10

God will send powerful servants to help gather His people unto Him

- Jacob 6:2

God will suffer with us, even when we are wicked

- Mosiah 8:20

When we stray, God will humble (or chasten) us until we return to Him

- Mosiah 12:4; 23:21

Christ will make us His children and heirs

- Mosiah 15:11

God will avenge us upon those who oppress us

- Mosiah 17:19

God will establish His people

- Mosiah 26:17; 3 Nephi 20:21

God will forgive us as often as we repent

- Mosiah 26:30

God will be quick to hear our cries and answer our prayers

- Alma 9:26

Christ will come to be among us with equity and justice in His hands

- Alma 10:21

God will work for our salvation in many ways

- Alma 24:27

Christ will suffer and die to atone for our sins

- Alma 33:22

God will help us see the works of darkness that the wicked are doing among us

- Alma 37:23

Christ will redeem us from our sins

- Helaman 5:10

God will prosper us

- Helaman 12:2

God will always remember to fulfill His covenant with us and give us a chance to have the gospel

- 2 Nephi 16:11; 3 Nephi 29:3

God will make us strong warriors

- 3 Nephi 20:19; 21:12

We will know that it is God who speaks to us
- 3 Nephi 20:39

When God gathers us, He will establish Zion among us
- 3 Nephi 21:1

God will bring the truth and a remembrance of His promises to us
- 3 Nephi 21:4; Doctrine and Covenants 3:19

We will be aided by non–covenant holders
- 3 Nephi 21:23

Non–covenant holders will help to gather God's covenant people
- 3 Nephi 21:24

We will be taught to call upon God in the name of the Son
- 3 Nephi 18:21

We will be taught about Christ
- Doctrine and Covenants 3:16

We will be blessed mightily
- Doctrine and Covenants 39:15; 41:1; 110:10

The riches of those who accept the covenant will be shared with the poor among the covenant
- Doctrine and Covenants 42:39; 78:3

Christ will be our king
- Doctrine and Covenants 76:63

Isn't it amazing how many blessings God has promised to covenant keepers? Further, isn't it incredible to see how many of these we can recognize by knowing that the scriptures about God's people are scriptures about people in a heightened relationship with God? Recognizing all the covenant phrases and ideas in the list above allows us to find more and more of the blessings promised to Israel. They are abundant in every volume of scripture.

Here is a short list of more of the promised blessings we can find when we look for textual cues that point toward the covenant concepts in the list above.

A Closer Relationship with God

God will lead us by the hand

- Abraham 1:18

God's power will be over us

- Abraham 1:18

God will be our God

- Genesis 17:7–8; Exodus 6:7; Leviticus 26:12; Deuteronomy 29:13; Abraham 1:19; 2:7

We will be God's people

- Exodus 6:7; Leviticus 26:12; Deuteronomy 7:6; 28:9–10; 29:13

We will be a peculiar treasure/special people to God

- Exodus 19:5

We will be a kingdom of priests and priestesses and a holy nation

- Exodus 19:6

God will set his tabernacle/temple among us and be with us

- Leviticus 26:11–12

God will extend a special mercy to those in the covenant

- Deuteronomy 7:9

We can be a prince/princess of peace

- Abraham 1:2

We will receive instructions

- Abraham 1:2

We will possess knowledge

- Abraham 1:2

God will put His name upon us through priesthood ordinances

- Abraham 1:18

A Closer Relationship with God Brings Blessings

God will prosper us (provide rain, abundant fruit, generous crop yields, increased flocks, full storehouses; all that we set our hand to will prosper, land will flow with milk and honey, we will be blessed beyond measure, etc.)

- Genesis 15:1; 17:6; Leviticus 25:18–19; 26:4–5; Deuteronomy 6:3; 28:3–6, 8, 11–12; 29:9; 30:9, 16; Abraham 2:9

We will be a blessing to our seed and the families of the earth

- Genesis 12:2–3; Abraham 2:9

We will bless all the earth

- Genesis 22:18; Abraham 2:10; Acts 3:25; 3 Nephi 20:25, 27; Galatians 3:8; Doctrine and Covenants 124:58

God will bless those that bless us

- Genesis 12:3; Abraham 2:11

God will curse those that curse us

- Genesis 12:3; Abraham 2:11

We will have a great name (among all nations)

- Genesis 12:2; Abraham 2:9

We will have our own kings/rulers

- Genesis 17:6, 16

All who receive the gospel will bless us

- Abraham 2:10

Priesthood ordinances will bless the world and give them a chance for salvation and eternal life

- Abraham 2:11

Blessings Include Protection

God will protect us

- Leviticus 25:18

We will possess the gates of our enemies

- Genesis 22:17; 24:60

God will be our shield

- Genesis 15:1

We will dwell safely

- Leviticus 25:18; 26:5

No evil beasts will be in our land/place

- Leviticus 26:6

No sword will go through our land/place

- Leviticus 26:6

We will chase our enemies, who will fall by the sword

- Leviticus 26:7

Five of Israel will chase 100, 100 will put 10,000 to flight, Israel's enemies will fall by the sword

- Leviticus 26:8

We will smite and chase our enemies in many directions

- Deuteronomy 6:19; 28:7

People will fear us

- Deuteronomy 28:10

We will lend and not borrow

- Deuteronomy 28:12

Amid the nations, we will be a head and not a tail, above and not beneath

- Deuteronomy 28:13

The Blessing of Posterity

We will be a great nation, and will be a mother/father of many nations

- Genesis 12:2; 17:4, 16

We will have seed as innumerable as the dust of the earth or the stars of heaven; God will multiply our seed; we will become a great nation

- Genesis 13:16; 15:5; 17:2, 4–6; 22:17; 24:60; Leviticus 26:9; Deuteronomy 6:3; 30:16; Abraham 2:9; 3:14

Our seed will continue for eternity
- Doctrine and Covenants 132:20–21

The covenant will be everlasting to us and our seed (even to a "thousand generations")
- Genesis 17:7; Deuteronomy 7:9; 1 Chronicles 16:15; Psalm 105:8

Through our ministry, God's name will be known throughout the earth
- Abraham 1:19

God's hand will be over us
- Abraham 2:8

We and our seed will bear ministry and priesthood ordinances to the world
- Abraham 2:9

All who receive the gospel will be called in our name and become our seed
- Abraham 2:10; Galatians 3:7, 29; 3 Nephi 30:2 (house of Israel in this case)

Our seed has a right to priesthood ordinances
- Abraham 2:11

We will receive eternal marriage and eternal continuation of seed
- Doctrine and Covenants 132:19

Getting Better at Recognizing the Blessings

Below we will list many of the blessings promised to Israel in the scriptures. But first, as part of helping you to develop your skills, we will ask you to look at a few specific chapters and make a list of the blessings promised to Israel that you find in those chapters. Then compare your list to my list for that same chapter. Of course, you will have found some things I did not, and I will have found some things you did not. Further, we will have thought of them or explained them in different ways. That is to be expected. The exercise of doing it on your own, then comparing it with what someone else has done will allow you to see things beyond what you would be able to see with only one set of eyes on the task. After doing this several times, you will find that you can more easily see the promised blessings throughout all the scriptures.

I suggest we start with a simple exercise. 1 Nephi 2:19–24 is where the Lord established the covenant with Nephi in a manner remarkably similar to the way it is outlined in Leviticus 26. I recommend reading those verses and making a list of the blessings promised therein, then comparing it to my list of blessings.

1 Nephi 2

They will prosper.
They will be led to a choice land of promise prepared for them (has symbolic celestial fulfillments as well).
They will receive protection from enemies.
Nephi and his descendants will be rulers and teachers.
God will help them return to Him when they stray.

Now let's practice by reading a longer chapter that speaks of the blessings of the covenant a number of times. Read 1 Nephi 10 and make a list of the blessings found therein. Frame the blessings in terms of what they are promising you. I also recommend writing down what these blessings might look like in your own life.

1 Nephi 10

God will bring us back when we have strayed or been punished.
We can possess choice promised lands we have lost due to sin or straying if we will return to God.
A Savior will be raised up to make this possible.
We can be redeemed from a lost and fallen state.
Prophets will help us come to this Redeemer so that we can be redeemed.
Prophets will help provide ordinances that allow us to access the covenant and redemption.

Prophets will bear record of the redeeming Messiah.
The gospel will be preached to covenant holders.
The gospel will be spread by the Holy Ghost.
In an effort to help them return to Him, God will humble covenant holders when they stray.
Covenant holders will be gathered to God again and have the opportunity to again access the Messiah's redemption.
God will reveal Himself to us when we seek Him through the Holy Ghost.

I recommend doing two more practice chapters. No scriptural writer focused on the covenant more than Isaiah, which was part of the reason Nephi loved him and quoted him extensively, and why the Savior so powerfully endorsed Isaiah's writings ("Great are the words of Isaiah," 3 Nephi 23:1). Let's look at two of the Isaiah chapters Nephi quoted and make a list of the blessings promised in those. Review 1 Nephi 20–21 / Isaiah 48–49 and see what you find.

1 Nephi 20 / Isaiah 48

We can be called by God's name.
God will spare us.
God will refine us.
God will speak to us.
God will prosper us.
God will teach us for our profit.
God will lead us.
God will love us.
We will have peace that flows as steadily as a river and righteousness that flows as powerfully and unendingly as the waves of the sea.
We can have innumerable offspring.
We can be redeemed.
God will provide for us in any kind of circumstance.

1 Nephi 21 / Isaiah 49

God will raise up prophets and a Messiah to guide us back to Him.

God will hear us.
God will help us.
God will preserve us.
We will inherit desolate places (which will become bountiful).
We will be delivered from all kinds of prisons.
We will be brought out of many forms of darkness into light.
We will be well cared for.
We will not hunger or thirst, and will be protected from harm.
God will have mercy on us.
God will lead us in the ways that bring peace and comfort.
Ways will be opened for us.
We will be gathered together and to God.
God will not forsake us.
God will not forget us.
God will always be thinking of us.
We will be protected from all that would harm us.
We will be surrounded and blessed by our offspring.
We will have innumerable offspring.
Others will help to bring us the blessings of offspring, and all the blessings of the covenant.
The powerful people and nations of the earth will do things that help to bless us and our families.
Kings and nations will bring about our prosperity (which can take several forms).
God will contend with everyone and everything that would harm us or our families.
God is powerful when He fights for us and redeems us.

More Blessings

Hopefully, everything we have done thus far enables you to have greater and greater success in recognizing the blessings promised to Israel as you read the scriptures. You will have many rich and rewarding experiences as you study the scriptures with this in mind. Over the next several years you will find that the list you compile will be so extensive as to be almost unwieldy.

In the meantime, here is a small list of some of the blessings promised to Israel as found in each book of scripture. The list is actually large, but compared to all the promised blessings found throughout all the scriptures, it is quite small.

We will be protected by the fact that people know that if they bless us they will be blessed, and if they curse us they will be cursed

- Genesis 12:3

God knows our sorrows and will deliver us

- Exodus 3:7–8

God will do wonders among us to deliver and protect us

- Exodus 3:20; Joshua 3:5

We can be courageous and fearless because God will not forsake us

- Deuteronomy 31:6

God will not forsake us

- 1 Samuel 12:22

God will have unending mercy upon us

- Deuteronomy 4:31

God will always preserve a remnant of the covenant people

- Isaiah 1:9

We can eat of the good of the land

- Isaiah 1:19

God will defend us from our oppressors

- Isaiah 10:17–18

God will continue to have mercy on us and choose us

- Isaiah 14:1

God will give us rest from our sorrow

- Isaiah 14:3

God will give us rest from our fear

- Isaiah 14:3

God will give us rest from our hard bondage
- Isaiah 14:3

God will take care of us when we are poor
- Isaiah 14:32

God will divert our enemies from us
- Isaiah 17:13

God will hear our cry and graciously answer us
- Isaiah 30:19

We will be comforted by God and His servants
- Isaiah 40:1

There is no reason to fear, for God will strengthen and uphold us
- Isaiah 41:10

We are God's
- Isaiah 43:1

God will make it easier for us to return to Him
- Isaiah 49:11; 62:10

God will cause leaders and nations of the world to help us accomplish His will
- Isaiah 49:22–23

We will be changed so that we can know God
- Jeremiah 24:7

We will be delivered from our oppressors and they will be punished
- Jeremiah 30:16

Ruin will be turned into prosperity for us
- Jeremiah 30:18

We will be multiplied and made great
- Jeremiah 30:19

God will always love us and will draw us to Him with loving-kindness
- Jeremiah 31:3

The covenant will become part of our newly begotten hearts
- Jeremiah 31:33

God will gather us from wherever we have been scattered
- Jeremiah 32:37

We will dwell safely in a place that belongs to us
- Jeremiah 32:37

We will be given a unified heart
- Jeremiah 32:39

Our hearts will be changed so that we won't want to turn away from God
- Jeremiah 32:40

God will rejoice in doing good things for us
- Jeremiah 32:41

God will be our sanctuary
- Ezekiel 11:16

Our hearts will be changed to have a more believing nature and capacity
- Ezekiel 11:19–20; 36:26

God will give us an everlasting covenant of peace
- Ezekiel 37:26

We will become changed, or become children of God
- Hosea 1:10; Doctrine and Covenants 45:7–9; John 1:12–13; Mosiah 5:6–7

God will be bound to us in love and mercy for forever
- Hosea 2:18–19

We will receive amazing abundance and love
- Hosea 14:4–8

God will heal us of our backsliding
- Hosea 14:4

God will love us freely
- Hosea 14:4

We will be saved by God's power

- Luke 1:69

We will receive mercy

- Luke 1:72–73

Christ will make sure that all promises to us are fulfilled

- Hebrews 7:22

God will dwell with us

- 2 Corinthians 6:16

We will be armed with the power of God in great glory

- 1 Nephi 14:14

We will be aided by others as we gather to our lands of inheritance and places of belonging

- 1 Nephi 22:6, 10–12

The covenant will be made available to us

- 1 Nephi 22:6, 9, 11

God will help us come off conqueror in the war against the great and abominable church

- 1 Nephi 22:13

We will be protected, sometimes by having the wicked destroy each other

- 1 Nephi 22:13–14, 18–19

The Book of Mormon will be brought to light to help restore the covenant and bring us to God

- 2 Nephi 29:1–2, 10–14

God will send prophets and Christ to nurture us and bring us back into the covenant

- Jacob 5

We will be delivered from bondage

- Alma 29:11–12

The covenant will be fulfilled, and we will eventually experience all its blessings

- 3 Nephi 15:8; 20:29–46; 22; 24:1–7, 17; 25:5–6; 29:3–9

We will receive our own promised land
- 3 Nephi 15:12–13; 20:14, 22

We will hear Christ's voice and have Him as our shepherd
- 3 Nephi 15:21

We will be numbered among those that the Father gives to the Son
- 3 Nephi 15:24; 16:3

We will be gathered
- 3 Nephi 16:5; 20:10–13, 18; 21:1–4; 28:28–29

Our seed will come to a knowledge of their Redeemer
- 3 Nephi 16:4

If we are scattered, others will bring the gospel to us
- 3 Nephi 16:6–10; 21:5–29; 26:8–10; 29:1–2

Christ will visit us to the fulfilling of all the Father's covenants with Israel
- 3 Nephi 11:14; 20:22–27

Our enemies will be cut off and we will come off conquerors
- 3 Nephi 20:16–17

We will be established
- 3 Nephi 20:21

We will have a promised land or place to live
- 3 Nephi 20:22

The powers of heaven will be in our midst
- 3 Nephi 20:22; 21:25

Christ will be in our midst
- 3 Nephi 20:22; 21:25

God will raise up prophets to guide us
- 3 Nephi 20:23

We will bless the whole earth
- 3 Nephi 20:25

Christ will come to turn us away from our iniquities

- 3 Nephi 20:26

God will remember the covenant He has made with us

- 3 Nephi 20:29

We will receive the fullness of the gospel

- 3 Nephi 20:30; 21:26

We will believe in Christ and pray to the Father in His name

- 3 Nephi 20:31; 21:27

We will be gathered unto the Father and sing for joy

- 3 Nephi 20:33–34

We will be made strong and beautiful and pure

- 3 Nephi 20:36

We shall be a free people

- 3 Nephi 21:4

Our prosperity and posterity will be magnified

- 3 Nephi 22:1–2

We will receive even more promised lands

- 3 Nephi 22:3

We will not be ashamed

- 3 Nephi 22:4

God's covenantal mercy will never depart from us

- Isaiah 54:10; 3 Nephi 22:10

We will be made into something beautiful and spectacular

- Isaiah 54:11–12; 3 Nephi 22:11–12

Our children will be taught of the Lord and will have great peace

- Isaiah 54:13; 3 Nephi 22:13

We will not need to fear because oppression will be kept far from us

- Isaiah 54:14; 3 Nephi 22:14

We will receive the Holy Ghost

- 3 Nephi 27:20

We will be sanctified by the Holy Ghost

- 3 Nephi 27:20

God will restore truths to help gather us

- Mormon 8:15

We will come to know of Christ and receive all covenantal blessings

- Mormon 9:36–37

We will be taught of our covenant identity

- Mormon 5:9

The house of Israel will be restored to the land of their inheritance

- Mormon 5:14

We will receive a remission of sins

- Moroni 10:33

God will reign in our midst and deliver us from the world

- Doctrine and Covenants 1:36

Our hearts will turn to our fathers and the covenant

- Doctrine and Covenants 2:2; Malachi 4:6

A knowledge of Christ will spread to the covenant people

- Doctrine and Covenants 3:16–20

We will be taught about God's promises and our covenant heritage and thus learn of Christ

- Doctrine and Covenants 3:20

Our descendants will have the true gospel preached to them

- Doctrine and Covenants 10:48–50

We will receive eternal life and inherit the kingdom of heaven

- Doctrine and Covenants 10:50–55

We and our descendants will receive the light of the gospel and true points of doctrine

- Doctrine and Covenants 10:61–62

God will unfold His mysteries to His covenant people
- Doctrine and Covenants 10:64

We will be gathered unto God and partake of the waters of life freely
- Doctrine and Covenants 10:65–66

The gates of hell will not prevail against us
- Doctrine and Covenants 10:69

We can become sons and daughters of God
- Doctrine and Covenants 11:30

We can have eternal life
- Doctrine and Covenants 14:7

We can have the Holy Ghost with us
- Doctrine and Covenants 14:8

We and our descendants will hear the gospel
- Doctrine and Covenants 14:10

We will always have His Spirit to be with us
- Doctrine and Covenants 20:77, 79

We will have peace in this world
- Doctrine and Covenants 59:23

We will receive eternal life in the next world
- Doctrine and Covenants 59:23

All things will be ours
- Doctrine and Covenants 76:59

We will come forth in the Resurrection of the just
- Doctrine and Covenants 76:65

We will be made perfect in Christ
- Doctrine and Covenants 76:69

We will receive celestial bodies
- Doctrine and Covenants 76:70

We will receive glory like God's
- Doctrine and Covenants 76:70

We will have refuge and defense from the storms of the last days

- Doctrine and Covenants 115:6

We will be redeemed according to the election of grace

- Doctrine and Covenants 84:99

We will receive priesthood ordinances, to which we have a right

- Doctrine and Covenants 86:8–11

Angels will watch over us

- Doctrine and Covenants 109:22

God will love us

- Doctrine and Covenants 109:61

God will gather us when we are scattered

- Doctrine and Covenants 109:61, 64

We can be sealed together

- Doctrine and Covenants 110:13–16

Summary of Promised Blessings

This list may seem relatively long; nevertheless, it is very incomplete. However, it is enough to make it clear that the voluminous blessings promised to covenant keepers are vast and overarching. It is difficult to keep track of how many blessings there are and how they can affect us. As you study the scriptures, if you keep in mind President Nelson's admonition and keep looking for the blessings promised to Israel, you will find your understanding of the scriptures will be greatly enhanced, and your ability to apply the scriptures to your life to be exponentially amplified. This is a lifetime pursuit, and I hope that we will never stop looking for these blessings throughout all our scripture study.

At the same time, the sheer number of promised blessings, and the scope of how thoroughly those blessings are scattered throughout scripture, can make it difficult for us to really wrap our head around those blessings. I believe it is helpful to be able to see a short summary of the most frequently repeated blessings. Here we will list them without the beautiful imagery that so often accompanies them. Rather, this list presents the most significant and frequently repeated blessings in a straightforward, plain, and simple manner. Covenant keepers will:

Develop a closer relationship with God.
Experience extended love and mercy.
Be gathered back to God no matter how often they stray from Him.
Be changed to become more like God.
Be protected.
Prosper mightily.
Have numerous posterity.
Have a place to belong, and a people with whom they belong.
Belong to God.
Be relieved of oppression.
Conquer their enemies in all their forms.
Be redeemed.
Be comforted.
Find peace.
Feel God's love and extend it to others.
Experience God's presence.
Be saved.
Be directed by God.
Experience miracles.
Be freed from bondage.
Be forgiven.
Be cleansed.
Be exalted.

All of this is possible because God loved us so much that He bound Himself to us and sent His Son to make it possible for these blessings to be fulfilled. Without the Father, Son, and Holy Ghost working in concert, we would not realize any of these blessings. With Them, these blessings and promises will be fulfilled in our lives in ways that surpass our current capacity to comprehend.

Staying on the Covenant Path

With such amazing promises attached to it, no wonder there is an increased and urgent emphasis on the spiritual significance of the covenant and its path. This has clearly been reiterated by President Nelson, who pleads with us to "keep on the covenant path. Your commitment to follow the Savior by making covenants with Him and then keeping those covenants will open the door to every spiritual blessing and privilege available to men, women, and children everywhere," including "the greatest gift of God—that of eternal life."[37]

But what exactly *is* the covenant path of which our leaders continually speak, and how do we know whether we are on it? To answer this, we should first explore the metaphor of a "path." The scriptures often use a path, or something similar, to describe the way back to God, which makes perfect sense. Our journey to return to God is not as much about arriving in a physical location as it is about changing our natures. Yet, our brains most easily conceive of any kind of journey in terms of getting from point A to point B. Thus, we talk about a strait and narrow path that leads us to God, and about an iron rod that helps us stay on that path. We speak of shepherds and guides who lead us through green pastures and help us come to a safe sheepfold. We talk about gates that both lead us to the right path and control access to it. We talk about a highway being cast up on which we can travel. Isaiah particularly makes use of this last image. It is worth exploring some of the ways Isaiah employs this symbol.

Isaiah speaks of a God creating a highway for a remnant of Israel on which they can return to Him, and compares it to the "way" He created for them as they left Egypt (see Isaiah 11:16). He later points out that the highways are unusable when someone who has broken the covenant attempts to travel on them (see Isaiah 33:8). When Isaiah next speaks of a highway, he describes one which will be called "the way of holiness," declaring that nothing unclean shall pass over it (see Isaiah 35:8). This almost sounds like

37 Russell M. Nelson, "As We Go Forward Together," *Ensign* or *Liahona*, April 2018, 7.

a description of the temple, with all of its covenant-administering ordinances. Another time, Isaiah speaks of a "way in the sea," and a "way in the wilderness" (Isaiah 43:16–20). In other places, Isaiah speaks of creating a path on which God's people can travel as they flock to a standard, or ensign (see Isaiah 49:11; 62:10). While it is possible that in all these verses Isaiah is speaking literally of roads and paths, it is almost certain that his primary emphasis is symbolic. He seems to repeatedly speak of a way to move forward that is clearly marked, makes travel toward God easy, and is a holy route. Isaiah often uses symbols to denote more than one thing,[38] which is likely what he is doing with the highway imagery. I am convinced that one of the primary meanings he intends for us to see behind the highway imagery is that God creates a covenant path that makes it possible for those who keep their promises to find their way back to God.

This notion of a symbolic path is potent. We tend to think of anything we want to do as a journey. We frequently use journey language to speak of things that are not literal journeys. For example, we use phrases like "steps," "paths," and "roadmaps" when we talk about trying to lose weight, figuring out educational and career goals, and a host of other things. Our brains intuitively understand journeys, and we naturally crave to have a clear path marked out for us whenever we think of travel. Thus, it is not surprising that the symbol for our process of returning to God is often spoken of in terms of a journey along a path.

But why are covenants so integrally tied to our journey to regain God's presence? While I am sure there are many answers to this question, here we will discuss only a few. First, this kind of forged bond creates the kind of relationship with God that both inspires us to keep moving toward Him and also allows Him to bless us with the power we need to continue that journey. Second, when we receive the power—or blessings—we need to continue our journey, if we receive them within a covenant context, then we can more easily keep in mind that these blessings are from God.

38 See Kerry Muhlestein, *Learning to Love Isaiah, A Guide and Commentary* (American Fork, UT: Covenant Communications, 2021), 7–8.

That, in turn, helps us to keep moving toward God rather than mistakenly believing that these blessings are the results of our own efforts, a prideful viewpoint that would inevitably lead us away from God. Avoiding this kind of pride is a never-ending struggle for all of God's children, but covenants can be a key component in avoiding pride. Third, covenants contain clear stipulations that provide measurable waypoints, or markers, allowing us to assess whether we are still on the path.

Entering the path by forging a covenant bond with God changes us. As President Nelson teaches, "When you and I enter that path, we have a new way of life. We thereby create a relationship with God that allows Him to bless and change us."[39] Our new natures and newly gained access to God's power allows us to progress on the path back to Him.

So, what are the markers that help us recognize whether we are still on the path? When experienced hikers travel along trails that are new to them, they often use both a GPS unit to help them know they are on the path, and they look for cairns, or piles of rocks, that those who have already traveled that path have created to mark the trail for others. God provides us with spiritual GPS markers and cairns as we travel the covenant path. We are already familiar with them; we just need to come to recognize them as the trail markers they are.

As Elder Bednar teaches, "Gospel covenants and ordinances operate in our lives much like a compass. A compass is a device used to indicate the cardinal directions of north, south, east, and west for purposes of navigation and geographic orientation. In a similar way, our covenants and ordinances point us to and help us always remember our connection with the Lord Jesus Christ as we progress along the covenant path."[40]

The beginning of the path is clearly marked. As you already know, we enter it through a gate—baptism. But have we really considered how effective that gateway is? It is when we are baptized that

39 Nelson, "The Everlasting Covenant."

40 Bednar, "But We Heeded Them Not," 15.

we enter into the Abrahamic—or new and everlasting—covenant. Remember that the covenant path is a way of holiness, and only those who are holy, or more like God and less like the world, can travel on that path. You might think of it as a spiritual HOV, or car-pool, lane in which only those who meet the right criteria can travel. The covenant we make at baptism makes us holy. If we have made that covenant with real intent, and if we have entered into it by the power of God and if it was administered by someone authorized to represent God in the covenant-making process, then our natures are changed at baptism. Our sins are washed away, and we become clean. Beyond that, as we receive the Holy Ghost, we are born again. The Holy Ghost carries the atoning power of Christ into our souls and sanctifies us. In other words, it changes us into holier beings—more like God and less fallen or worldly. At this point we are on the covenant path, we have become godlier, and thus we are more capable of a higher relationship with God.

The way to move forward is marked by the terms of the covenant. We promise that we will obey God's commands and bear witness of Him. Above all else, we promise to love God and draw ever closer to Him, and to love and take care of each other. The covenant path consists of our fulfilling our promised obligations. If we want to know whether we are on this path, we need only ask ourselves two questions: 1) Am I striving to do what I promised God I would do? 2) Am I working toward the next step—or covenant—on the path? In other words, are we striving to live our lives according to the gospel, and are we loving God and each other? It does not mean that we are perfect in our obedience—no one is. It means that we are *striving* to live the right way. If we are trying to obey and love, then we are on the path. If we are working toward making covenants in the temple, which is the next step on the path after baptism, then we are safely on the path. If we are doing things that would prevent us from going to the temple, then we are not on the path. Note that in a temple recommend interview, besides faith-affirming questions, we are asked two kinds of questions: We are asked about whether we are doing things that would remove us from the covenant path, such as disobedience to God's laws. We are also asked if we are *striving* to live His laws and to do things that are in accordance with loving God and each other.

As just mentioned, the next step, or waypoint, in the path is to undertake these solemn promises in the temple. There we are washed and anointed,[41] which conveys symbolism similar to that of baptism; for we wash away the sins of the world and are anointed to become something more than we were beforehand, which allows us to become even more godly. This in turn makes us capable of an even closer relationship with Him. We also make further promises to obey, follow, love, and serve God, and also to love each other and care for each other. Each of these promises helps increase our godliness both in terms of how we act and how fully we can be changed by Christ. Our new and godlier natures then enhance our upward spiral toward our relationship with God.

If, with covenant consciousness of our desire to have a closer relationship with God, we learn about Christ and try to emulate Him, we will find amplified blessings flowing into our lives. Emulating Christ naturally fills us with a greater love for God and His Son. This creates an upward spiral, because experiencing such an enhanced love will lead to an increased desire to live in a godly manner. This increased desire inevitably heightens our emulation of Christ. Further, we will better understand what a godly walk, or behavior, looks like because we will have seen it in the way Christ behaved. Following Christ's example means we will serve others; therefore, we will also start to naturally love others more, which changes our nature to be more like Christ's. Further, this increased love of God and men, combined with a godlier behavior, will intensify our bond with God, which will cause us to be more open to the Spirit in our lives. This allows God to change our nature to be even more Christlike.

To be clear, this edifying pattern consists of the following elements: 1) We love God. 2) We covenant with God. 3) We follow

41 See Joseph Smith, "History, 1838–1856, volume C-1 [2 November 1838–31 July 1842]," 1328, *The Joseph Smith Papers*, accessed July 1, 2022, https://www.josephsmithpapers.org/paper-summary/history-1838-1856-volume-c-1-2-november-1838-31-july-1842/502.

the example of His Son because we love God and have promised to act in a Christlike way. 4) Our natures change because of the covenant and the way we act. 5) We then experience a higher love for God and His Son. 6) We have an increased desire to emulate Christ because of this love. 7) We serve others more as we lovingly emulate Christ. 8) We love others more as a result of serving them. 9) Our natures are changed even further because of our heightened love for others. 10) This edified nature creates in us an increased capacity to love God, starting the spiral over again.

Thus, focusing on learning of and loving Christ, or the Way, will exponentially increase our spiritual momentum along the covenant path as we spiral upward toward union with God. As a result, it is helpful to sometimes think of the covenant path as a covenant spiral. We can spiral up or down that path, depending upon how well we focus on and keep the covenant. Spiraling upward exponentially strengthens bonds with God, which we forged by entering into His covenant. Focusing on ourselves and ascribing the blessings we receive to our own abilities and efforts causes us to spiral away from God.

Fortunately, we have the opportunity to renew our covenants regularly and thus keep ourselves in the center of the covenant path. We symbolically do so as we return to the temple to help those on the other side of the veil have the opportunity to enter into these same covenants. Performing proxy covenantal work for the dead allows us to review our own promises. Hopefully, we renew those covenants in our hearts at the same time we make them for others. We *actually* renew them weekly as we partake of the sacrament. As Elder Adeyinka A. Ojediran teaches, "In staying faithful to our covenants, we should endeavor to always have the Spirit to prepare us to worthily partake of the sacrament, and likewise, we regularly partake of the sacrament to always have the Spirit with us."[42] Covenant renewal allows us to take stock of how well we are staying on the path. If the Spirit is with us, not only is that a good waypoint indicating we are on the path, but it helps us

42 Adeyinka A. Ojediran, "The Covenant Path: The Way to Eternal Life," *Liahona*, May 2022, 106.

recognize ways we can either course correct or press forward more firmly. If the Spirit seems to have withdrawn from our lives, that is akin to recognizing we no longer see the cairns that mark the path. We should then hurry back to the marked path by means of repentance.

If we do indeed keep our covenants, we can move toward the next step on the path, which is to be sealed in the temple. Temple weddings, or being sealed together as a family, are clearly about the Abrahamic covenant. This is especially true in terms of having numerous posterity. As President Nelson teaches, "Think of it! A marriage made in the temple is tied directly to that Abrahamic covenant. In the temple, a couple is introduced to *all* the blessings reserved for the faithful posterity of Abraham, Isaac, and Jacob."[43]

We can ask ourselves if we are on the covenant path by asking if we are keeping the promises we have already made, and if we are avoiding those things that would make it so that we cannot renew our covenants or move toward the next step. If we are staying worthy of making our next set of covenants, or are staying worthy of renewing those promises, we are on the path. If we are doing something that would make us unworthy to partake of more covenants, or unworthy to renew our covenants, we are straying from the path. Further, as just noted, the companionship of the Holy Ghost, or the loss of it, helps us know whether we are on the path. Fortunately, the power of the covenant itself helps us stay on the path and recognize when we are straying. As President Nelson has taught, "Those who keep their covenants with God will become a strain of sin-resistant souls! Those who keep their covenants will have the strength to resist the constant influence of the world."[44]

This highlights another aspect of the covenant path. One interesting marker of whether or not we are on the path is whether we are "peculiar" (Exodus 19:5), or more like God and less like the world. In other words, the covenant path is not the path the world takes, and often, those who are on the path will feel a tension with

43 Nelson, "The Everlasting Covenant," 6; emphasis original.

44 Nelson, "The Everlasting Covenant," 8.

the world. Some of this tension will come because the world wants us to think of ourselves differently than God does. As President Nelson has recently emphasized, our primary identities should be 1) we are children of God, 2) we are children of the covenant, and 3) we are disciples of Christ and members of His restored Church. That is not how the world thinks of us. When we find ourselves thinking of other self-identities more than these, we should recognize those thoughts as a warning that we are starting to stray from the covenant path. If we are filtering all other ways we think of ourselves through these identities, we can take that as a sign that we are on the path.

Similarly, if we feel uncomfortable with a number of things the world is teaching, we are probably moving along the covenant path. If we encounter ideas of the world that run contrary to the teachings of the prophet and we side with the world, deciding that the prophets and apostles just don't quite understand, that is a pretty good sign that we are starting to wander from the path.

Following prophets, both ancient and modern, is an important marker on the covenant path. When we combine what we have learned in the scriptures about the covenant with our desire to stay on the covenant path, we find another powerful tool for helping us make sure we remain on the path. As we recognize when prophets in the scriptures are talking about the covenant, and when we recognize that we, too, are covenant Israel, we will find that these prophets offer us dozens upon dozens of cairns to help us make sure we are on the path. All we have to do is take a moment to ask ourselves if we are on the right side of the waypoints they have laid out for us.

For example, if we recognize that the Old Testament prophet Amos was preaching to Israel and warning them that they were straying from the path and that if they didn't return, they would be punished and scattered, then we realize that his teachings were also about ways that modern Israel is straying from the path. Thus, when he warns us that we sell the poor for a pair of shoes (see Amos 2:6; 8:6), we should ask ourselves how it applies to us. Are there ways we are selling the poor for a pair of shoes? Perhaps this means that if I am buying a pair of shoes I don't really need instead of taking care of my fellow Saints in need, I am not keeping the covenant the way I should. Surely as a covenant keeper I am to love my neighbors and care for them, so am I more in love with a flashy but unnecessary pair of shoes (or some other luxury) than I am with my neighbor? This question may be difficult to wrestle with and can be answered in many ways. *Asking* the question will help keep us firmly on the covenant path, regardless of how we end up *answering* it. This is just one example of how we can recognize scriptural teachings about the covenant and then make those teachings a waypoint check as to how firmly we are on the covenant path. With this mindset and the skills to recognize covenant language, we will find that the scriptures are an intense spiritual GPS system for making sure we stay on the covenant path.

Yet there is a danger from over-analyzing the waypoints of the covenant path, and it can be a paralyzing error if we allow that to happen. One mistake we often make is to confuse the covenant path with a self-created list of things we need to be doing. Undoubtedly, those who are truly on the path will be busy doing many good things. But the path does not consist of a to-do list, not even a scripture-generated to-do-list. If it did, we would all fail in our journey along the path because none of us is a perfect list-keeper, and none of us can check off everything on a list—meaning we will never do enough things to come to the end of the path.

Fortunately, staying on the path consists of keeping in the Way. Jesus Christ is the Way. Everything stems from this truth. If we are on the covenant path, each of us is giving up our old self. In its place, we each receive a new, Christ-created self—we become new creatures in Christ (see 2 Corinthians 5:17; Mosiah 27:26). That new self is suffused with a love of God and a love of His children. Being children of God who love Him becomes our primary identity and shapes the way we view and feel about everything in life. For each of us, our love of God will generate a host of things we desire to accomplish. The scriptures and the Spirit will guide us in prioritizing our desires. This is not a checklist for exaltation; rather it is a desire to do more and more things that are a natural expression of loving God and loving our neighbor. We will want to do more than we are capable of doing. This should not cause us concern, for we know that over time—even over eons of time—our capacities to do more will increase. Currently, we need to know that we don't approach God by doing everything on a list, no matter how righteous that list is and how well it coincides with what we are reading in the scriptures. It is important for us to realize that the cairns and waypoints of the path are not in a self-generated to-do list. Rather than checking to see if we are on the path by asking whether we are crossing things off a list, we should ask ourselves if we love God more than anything, and if we love His children. If we find anything in our lives competing with our love of God, we should beware that we may be straying from the path. Rather, our love for God, and the communion that comes from that love, will create a set of desires we will naturally work on fulfilling. We will find ourselves fully consecrated to God in a passionate way that can only grow from our great love for Him. If we are acting out of love, we are then surely on the covenant path. Acting for other motives tends to cause us to stray from that path. If the *primary and most prevalent and significant* way we think of ourselves is as children of God who love Him, then we can recognize that characteristic as the most important cairn indicating we are on the right path.

Another indicator that we are on the covenant path is whether we find ourselves feeling a love for others. Creating a closer relationship with each other is also part of the covenant. As President Jean B. Bingham teaches, "As [people] who make and keep covenants with God, we share spiritual bonds that help us meet the challenges of our day and prepare us for the Second Coming of Jesus Christ."[45] Feeling a love for others and a desire to strengthen bonds with them and help and uplift them is a cairn, or marker,

45 Jean B. Bingham, "Covenants with God Strengthen, Protect, and Prepare Us for Eternal Glory," *Liahona*, May 2022, 66.

that can help us recognize we are still on the path. Having a desire to end conflict and create more peace and love in our relationships, as President Nelson has asked us to do, is another waypoint that indicates we are on the covenant path of loving each other.[46] "The greatest joy you will ever experience is when you are consumed with love for God and for all His children. Loving God more than anyone or anything else is the condition that brings true peace, comfort, confidence, and joy."[47]

Because the covenant hinges upon God's desire for us to have a closer relationship with Him, the simplest GPS measurement as to whether we are on the path is to ask this question: Am I doing things that draw me closer to God, things that increase my relationship with Him? If so, you are on the covenant path. If your relationship is growing more distant, it is akin to no longer seeing the cairns that mark the path. That is a time to hurry back to the waypoint of loving God and letting Him prevail in your life.

Fortunately, one crucial element of the covenant is that God is *always* willing to accept us back when we stray. In both Leviticus 26 and Deuteronomy 28–30—the two places where this divine agreement is most clearly outlined—the explanation of the covenant, its blessings, and the consequences that come from breaking it are followed by a clear statement of God's willingness to accept us back into the covenant whenever we have strayed. This mirrors President Nelson's teachings that when we stray from the path we can repent and return to the path.[48] President Nelson emphasized that we have never strayed so far that we cannot repent and regain the path. As Sister Amy A. Wright teaches, "[Jesus] can heal broken relationships with God, broken relationships with others, and broken parts of ourselves."[49] Thus, the happy news is that anytime we detect we are not full of love for God, or that we are doing things that cause us to draw further away from Him rather than closer, we can always

46 See Nelson, "The Power of Spiritual Momentum," 97.

47 Nelson, "The Everlasting Covenant," 11. Also see Muhlestein, *God Will Prevail,* 119–121 and 127–129.

48 See Nelson, "The Power of Spiritual Momentum," 99.

49 Amy A. Wright, "Christ Heals That Which Is Broken," *Liahona,* May 2022, 82.

come back to the path. Christ came to make it possible for the covenant to change our fallen nature into a godly nature, and also to make it possible for us to rejoin the covenant path when we have strayed.

The covenant path is not about whether we are enough or do enough. It is a path about what we can become in Christ. It is a path of love. The things we do and the things we become flow from the love we feel *for* others, the love we feel *from* others, and the relationships created by that love, most especially the enabling relationship with Christ that creates a new you.

Yes, the covenant path is a path of love.[50] It is also a path of incredible, unimaginable blessings. How blessed we are to be children of an Almighty Being who loves us and is willing to bind Himself to us! How fortunate we are to live in a day where we have modern prophets whom God is asking to remind us of this bond! How wonderful that the ordinances and covenants are available to us in these, the last days! How grateful we should be that the path that binds us to God is so clearly marked and readily accessible! Above all, how sublime it is that God has established this binding and edifying covenant with us and then sent His Son, who makes it possible for the covenant to be fulfilled!

---

50 Muhlestein, *God Will Prevail*, 119; and Nelson, "The Everlasting Covenant," 11.

About the Author

Kerry Muhlestein is a professor and former associate chair of the Department of Ancient Scripture at Brigham Young University, where he has taught about the Abrahamic Covenant for almost three decades. He received his BS in psychology with a Hebrew minor from BYU, his MA in Ancient Near Eastern studies from BYU, and his PhD from UCLA in Egyptology with a secondary emphasis in Hebrew language and literature. He is also the director of the BYU Egypt Excavation Project, and his family has lived in Jerusalem on multiple occasions while Kerry has taught there. He and his wife, Julianne, are the parents of six children and grandparents to one grandson.